THE
DEVIL'S
SECRETS

What He Doesn't Want You to Know

D. BROOKS BAKER

Copyright © 2013 by D. Brooks Baker
All rights reserved.

ISBN: 146636453X
ISBN 13: 9781466364530

Library of Congress Control Number: 2013920294
CreateSpace Independent Publishing Platform
North Charleston, South Carolina

For Annie

You gave me time to find myself. You gave me a family so I could learn what's really important. But most of all, you gave me unconditional love, something I had only thought possible in fairy tales. I love you.

Contents

Chapter		Page
1.	The Powers Against Us	1
2.	The Family	5
3.	Pride	11
4.	Mothers	16
5.	Fathers	21
6.	Children	26
7.	Religion	30
8.	Light and Darkness	36
9.	Prayer	43
10.	Obedience	48
11.	Addiction	53
12.	Alcohol and Drugs	57
13.	Pornography	63
14.	Hope	68
15.	The Devil	72
16.	The Holy Spirit	77
17.	The Word of God	81
18.	Jesus and You	86
19.	The Devil's End	94

*And the great dragon was cast out,
that old serpent,
called the Devil, and Satan,
which deceiveth the whole world:
he was cast out into the earth,
and his angels were cast out with him.
—Revelation 12:9*

Chapter One

The Powers Against Us

He stood before his dark-hearted legion,
A smile upon his face,
For his power had never been greater
Over the human race.

Nations and armies and leaders of men
Were at his beck and call,
And it wasn't an overstatement to say
That the Devil was having a ball.

The war he was waging was taking its toll,
And yes, it was going quite well,
By the hundreds, the thousands, and even the millions
He was leading mankind to hell.

But there are secrets that must remain
Or they would ruin his sinister plan,
For if God's children learned what the Devil knew
He'd lose his power over man.

So with arms outstretched, "Onward!" he yelled.
"Onward to victory!
And we must strike at God's very heart
And destroy the family!"

Secret One

*The first truth Satan seeks to hide
Is that the choice is up to you,
That he cannot make you do anything
You don't agree to do.
Yes, he's had several thousand years
To prepare and lead you astray,
And he has a million subtle tricks
He'll use to pull you his way.
But every choice is entirely yours,
You're free to do as you please,
Though the fruit of all the choices you make
Will be the person you come to be.*

You don't choose your family.
They are God's gift to you,
as you are to them.
—Desmond Tutu

Chapter Two

The Family

*"What God so loves, let us tear asunder,
The husband, the wife, and the child.
Our attack must begin in the home,"
Satan said with a sinister smile.*

*"Mankind mustn't see the strength of families
That follow the Father and Son,
So we must work to pull them apart
Before they, with God, become one.*

*"And how will we do this?" the Devil asked,
His minions, watching their king.
"We'll whisper that they should spend their hearts
Seeking worldly things.*

"If somehow things become their treasure,"
The thought almost made him laugh,
"They'll forget about God and loving each other,
And worship their golden calf.

"We'll wrap these trinkets up really pretty,
And make them seem so worthwhile,
And as families covet these stale pots of porridge
They'll be ignorant of our guile.

"We know God wants the best for mankind,
For them to have the bounties of earth,
But believing that things are what life's about
Is a lie to which we must give birth.

"We'll use two gifts God's given man:
Their intelligence and desire to create.
And everything they design for their good
We will work to contaminate!

"Radio, television, and the computer,
I tell you, the list is quite long.
All that they invent and discover,
We'll put our dirty mark on.

"We're already in their music.
We're twisting the songs that they sing,
Until even I'm surprised at the power
We've gained over that one thing.

"Radio is taking our words to the world,"
He said, enjoying the thought.
"And as we hide my doctrine in song
They don't even know they're being taught.

"Now the words many sing from the heart,
Are those we most want to hear.
The world resounds with vulgarity and lust."
And the Devil's angels cheered.

He then added, "Don't forget television.
We know how useful it can be.
But now that it's mostly in my control,
It's leading millions to me.

"We started off ever so slowly,
By placing one little toe in the door,
And now we've filled their minds with trash,
And left them begging for more.

"And the computer, along with its Internet,
Immerses millions in filth every day.
Click after click, conscience is numbed
And it brings so many my way.

"This tool has opened a door to the home
That we never had in the past,
And unless good parents are ever so careful
We'll drag them, with their children, down fast.

"There are houses, cars, and boats,
And wireless inventions not thought of.
Our job is to make these things their desire,
And what they most deeply love.

"And by tempting them to live beyond their means
And yearn for heartless possessions,
We'll pull good parents away from the home
And their families in my direction.

"It's things, it's things, it's things, I say,
That must become their treasure.
And as mankind covets these silly things
My desire will become their pleasure."

Secret Two

The Devil's Second Secret is this:
When a family is centered on Christ,
The Holy Spirit envelops their home,
Strengthening their desire to do right.
Through Jesus, families will cease to covet
The Devil's counterfeit treasure,
And their hearts will yearn for eternal things,
For riches that last forever.

*Pride gets no pleasure
out of having something,
only out of having more of it
than the next man.
—C. S. Lewis*

Chapter Three

Pride

The Devil's plan is working quite well,
Though it must be moved speedily along,
Because time is quickly running out
To tempt God's children to do wrong.

His workers must push harder,
Yes, they must pick up the pace,
And inspire one of his favorite old sins
If they're to trap the human race.

"We must immerse them in pride," Satan said,
"Of how one can be better than another.
And with worldly things we can easily pit
A brother against his brother.

"The more you have, the greater you are,
Is a lie quite easy to hatch.
And as we fill the world with selfish pride,
Oh, the number of God's children we'll catch.

"And the wonderful thing about wounded pride
Is the value of the act rarely matters.
People have been killed over principles and pennies,
And that's definitely something I'm after.

"Some will even believe they're better
Because of the color of their skin."
The Devil laughed, his arms outstretched,
"And that's one of my favorite sins.

"It doesn't matter how selfish pride is manifest,
So long as it's in their heart.
For when pride's on the loose, it doesn't take long
To tear a nation apart.

"To think of all of pride's uses:
Wars, prejudice, and hate.
Societies have fallen from this one little sin,
Which is what makes pride so great."

As if on cue, his cronies applauded.
They truly could not agree more.
For with pride raging, dragging man to hell
Isn't really that difficult a chore.

To the joy of his throng, the Devil then added,
"It can't be made any clearer.
Selfish pride makes the god men worship
The one staring back from the mirror."

Secret Three

*The Third Secret comes as a lie.
Satan says selfish pride is okay,
For he knows that this one little flaw
Makes it easier to pull you his way.
Even more, he seeks to hide
The cure for this self-centered sin.
For the longer you cuddle with selfish pride
The better it is for him.
But the balm is the second great commandment,
To love your neighbor as yourself.
And the Devil knows, if we'll just love each other,
He'll be very lonely in hell.*

*Only God Himself
fully appreciates the influence
of a Christian mother
in the molding of character
in her children.
—Billy Graham*

Chapter Four

Mothers

*The Devil pointed to his army
As they silently and eagerly looked on,
Saying, "We must attack the mother's role
And make it seem like something bygone.*

*"The qualities possessed by the gentler sex
Must be put to an end, and quick,
Because the thought of a virtuous woman
Just about makes me sick.*

*"We must whisper of a counterfeit greatness,
One that's found on a business card,
And as worldly things become their treasure
This really won't be all that hard.*

"But to ensure they're fully persuaded,
We'll suggest that the male reigns supreme,
And that bearing and nurturing children
Is an inconvenient thing."

The Devil paused, his minions waiting
For the rest of his plan to unfurl,
Then he hissed, "If we get to the mothers,
We will own the world.

"But we'll have to go after them young,
Go after every single little girl child.
We don't want them growing up good,
We want them to be girls gone wild.

"A young woman must use her body,
The temple with which she's been blessed,
As a thing for the world to ogle.
And we can do this through vile contests,

"Until all that was precious and pure
Is nothing but a spoiled piece of meat.
Then we'll have won a key battle,
And oh, won't that victory be sweet.

*"Yes, we must attack God's daughters
With all the power that we can muster,
And if things go as I'm hoping,
God's work will truly be flustered."*

Secret Four

Secret Four asks, why does Satan
Attack God's daughters with such might?
The answer is, that a virtuous woman
Is impossible for him to fight.
Rubies, diamonds, and even gold
Will never, ever come close
To the gift of a righteous mother
And the influence that she holds.
So let God's daughters say in their hearts,
"I am Jesus's girl,"
Because the world needs virtuous women
If good is to win the world.

*A man ought to live so that
everybody knows he is a Christian…
and most of all
his family ought to know.*
—*Dwight L. Moody*

Chapter Five

Fathers

"Let's not forget about Dad," said the Devil,
"Or all the good he can do.
As with Mother, we must steer him from God,
Yes, we must distract him, too.

"Even without our sinister efforts
A father's job is quite enormous,
So we must promote all but Christ in his life,
And pull him straight to us.

"We'll use his desire to bless his family,
And turn it to our designs.
We'll whisper, 'Things are what your children need,
Not their father's time.'

"We'll keep him so burdened by cares of the world,
He'll forget the greater prize,
That real value isn't found from nine to five,
But is reflected in his child's eyes.

"And as we pull Dad away from the home
Under the pretense of making lives better,
We'll slowly turn him to worldly things,
And from the riches of forever.

"And as you've seen, we can often get them
Before they become husbands at all,
By having our wild girls fill their desires,
Thus muting the marriage call.

"We'll also whisper that power over others
Is the measure of a man's success.
And while exerting unrighteousness dominion,
It won't be personal, just business.

"And as Daddy becomes entrapped by cares
That are far from his Savior's heart,
He'll be caught in my deadly grasp
And I'll tear his family apart.

*"How wonderful it is when children lose faith
In the man that leads their home,
Because it's hard to believe in a Father above
When your earthly father roams.*

*"Like Mother, there are few things greater
Than a father his children can trust.
So, for my plan to be successful,
Destroying dear Daddy's a must."*

Secret Five

*Satan wants nothing more
Than to bury Secret Five,
Which is, homes without Christ-like fathers
Are easier for him to divide.
Earth's most fertile garden spot
For nurturing the eternal soul
Is within the walls of a Christ-centered home,
Where divine nature grows.
Father, remind yourself daily
That, while you protect and provide,
Your time, your witness, and your love
Is what lights your child's eyes.
Worldly treasures and earthly castles
Will one day no longer be,
But love's sweet harvest from garden home,
Will bear fruit for eternity.*

*There can be no keener revelation
of a society's soul
than the way in which it treats
its children.*
—Nelson Mandela

Chapter Six

Children

*"The child, the child," said the Devil.
"We must somehow get to the child.
We must attack them while they're young.
The child must grow up wild.*

*"If we can stain their early years
And lead them from God's holy ways,
There's a very good chance we'll own them
The remainder of their days.*

*"We know that the punishment's grim
For those offending the little ones of the Lord.
A millstone to hell if they don't repent,
Where their cries will forever be heard.*

"But there's a bonus in wronging a child,
Far beyond the transgressor's lost soul.
For when a child is shattered at a young age,
It's hard for that child to be whole.

"Often, they'll stop trusting others,
And blame their Father above.
And anger like that makes it hard to feel
Their Savior's unconditional love.

"Yes, we must corrupt their early years,
Then whisper that they should just give in.
Why even try when it started so badly?
Make them quit before they even begin."

Secret Six

*The most sordid of the Devil's secrets
May possibly be Number Six,
For if employed as he desires
It's very difficult to fix.
He seeks to spoil each child of God
While in their tender days,
And if successful, he's almost assured
The power to pull them his way.
So let us protect our little ones
With more care than diamonds and gold,
For if so guarded they'll become
Christ's disciples as they grow old.
Let us protect our babes from evil,
Teach them to be obedient and wise,
Then the world will become the joyous place
As seen through a child's eyes.*

*Preach the Gospel at all times,
and when necessary,
use words.
—Francis of Assisi*

Chapter Seven

Religion

*The Devil surveyed his dreadful throng,
Then said with an ice-cold stare,
"If we can somehow pollute religion,
We'll catch many in our snare.*

*"Millions are walking the narrow way
That leads to the one true God,
So we must use our tools to move them
From the safety of gospel sod.*

*"We'll take an interest in those," he added,
"Who have heeded the Master's call,
And once they become ministers of Christ,
We'll attack them with our all.*

*"It's true, we won't seduce many.
The numbers will be relatively few.
But it only takes one in a hundred or so
To do what we need them to do.*

*"If we trap a few of their shepherds
In sins of deceit and lust,
Many sheep will become lost,
And wander straight to us.*

*"But other benefits come from demeaning
Those who teach the words of the Master.
Millions will no longer trust religion,
And what a wonderful disaster.*

*"We'll also inspire progressive morals,
And through laws, God's influence we'll negate,
While whispering that faith in Christ
Mustn't mix with affairs of the state.*

*"We know it's not what the founders intended
When they put the Constitution to pen.
Even John Adams said it was only fit
To govern moral and religious men.*

"We must remove God from their schools,
At least the god that leads men to Christ,
For when a Christ-less nation makes the rules
Its people pay a terrible price.

"And we must work to turn their faith
Into a club, rather than a light.
We want them to focus on hell and damnation,
Rather than love, as the reason to do right.

"We'll also inspire gossip,
For when loosed among Christ's people,
It drives many into the lone wilderness,
And from beneath the church's safe steeple.

"Even now, millions believe
That religion is for weak-minded folk,
And instead of their Savior's light burden
They're being saddled with my terrible yoke.

"Yes, we must corrupt the churches,
And make man believe that it's better
To worship in solitary confinement,
That their faith may be practiced unfettered.

*"And as we pull them from the congregations,
Like a lone coal removed from the fire,
They'll lose the warm, comforting witness of friends,
Which often motivates righteous desires.*

*"Their need for religion must cease!" Satan yelled.
"Gathering together must appear naïve.
Then you'll be surprised at how very quickly
Fewer and fewer will believe."*

Secret Seven

*The Devil has been quite successful
In using Secret Seven
To pull mankind in his direction
And from the God of heaven.
He whispers in mankind's ears,
"You must be perfect to be a Christian,
And those who aren't are hypocrites,
If they teach the Savior's doctrine."
What the Devil fails to reveal
Is that the church is a healing place,
Filled with sinners bearing spiritual wounds
In need of their Savior's grace.
Perfect people need not apply
To carry the Christian card,
But the doors are open for all who seek
Christ's healing with all their heart.*

*Darkness cannot drive out darkness;
only light can do that.
Hate cannot drive out hate;
only love can do that.
—Dr. Martin Luther King Jr.*

Chapter Eight

Light and Darkness

The Devil surveyed his underlings
As they counseled over the souls of man.
His scheme, seeming steadfast and sure,
Though he knew it was a fragile plan.

Success relied upon mankind choosing
His darkness over Christ's holy light.
Man must settle for endless damnation,
Instead of eternal life.

It continued to astound the old serpent
That he could lead so many to transgression,
When the gentle voice of the Holy Spirit
Made such an indelible impression.

Yet like lemmings they continued to follow,
Over the murky edge,
Dancing to the wicked Pied Piper's tune,
Till to him, their souls they had pledged.

And the war would continue, he'd never give up,
For it was God who had cast him out.
He'd drag as many to hell as he could,
Yes, revenge is what this is about.

And he knew he was making an impact
Upon his demonic throng,
But if his sinlings didn't push hard
So many things could go wrong.

They needed to attack the principles
At the center of the Father's plan,
And make Christ's teachings seem foolish
Or they'd lose the hearts of man.

He was worried first about faith
And the power that it possessed.
And he knew that few understood it,
Or how through it their lives could be blessed.

*"Faith of a mustard seed!" the Devil hissed.
"If the children of God only knew,
That if it became affixed in their souls,
There's no limit to what they could do!*

*"And we all know that faith is greatest
In those who obey the Savior,
So to weaken this gift, we must work harder
At corrupting mankind's behavior.*

*"Faith in God must be made to seem
As the suggestion of a foolish man.
We'll tell them it's just a silly old notion,
At least, that's the plan.*

*"They mustn't learn that faith is the key
To receiving all that they want and need;
And that heaven's angels eagerly wait
To help each child of God succeed."*

*The Devil then moved on to another principle
That had him worried, as well.
"Repentance must not be used," he threatened,
"Or we'll never drag anyone to hell.*

"I despise the idea of forgiveness,
Of how Jesus can make men clean.
No, I want sins red as scarlet,
Not Isaiah's pure-as-snow scheme!

"To think of all that we're doing
To lead God's children astray,
Then along comes the gift of repentance,
And in a moment our work's washed away.

"There's nothing that I hate more
Than Christ's redeeming blood.
How can sin and corruption compete
With the Savior's perfect love?

"Forgiveness must seem impossible.
Men must believe their sins are too great.
They must be made to truly feel
That repentance for them is too late.

"You've blown it, you're done, you're just a bad seed,
Are lies we'll strive to spread.
My goal is simple, delay the healing
Until the mortal man is dead.

"Yes, we must bury repentance,
We must strike it to the ground,
Before God's children employ the miracle,
Are forgiven, and eternally crowned."

Secret Eight

"Darkness, leave, you aren't welcome,"
Comes the sinner's prayer.
Yet on the morrow the gutter beckons
And he finds himself wallowing there.
But in Secret Eight a lesson is learned:
Darkness can't tolerate the Light,
And the anguished soul draws back the curtain
With all his heart and might.
For the Son, the Light, to whom he belongs,
Can remove darkness from his soul,
And where shadows once were thought to reign,
The Light makes the child of God whole.

*The trouble with our praying is,
we just do it as a means of last resort.*
—Will Rogers

Chapter Nine

Prayer

A powerful gift has been given to man,
Even a tool, known as prayer.
And because it links us directly to God,
It's something Satan strives to impair.

He raised his arms, frustrated, saying,
"How can I fight this spiritual connection?
Ask and receive, it's been made too simple
To call upon the Father's affection.

"Man mustn't learn that fervent prayer
Is a key to real spiritual strength,
And to hide this powerful, precious truth,
I will go to any length.

"It's been said, when you don't feel like praying
Is the time that you most need to pray,
But we'll whisper, 'If you don't feel like praying,
Put it off for another day.'

"If mankind will only procrastinate prayer,
Or even stop communicating with God,
Then alone and relying upon themselves,
They'll be forced through life to trod.

"And if they'll heed our enticing
And walk through life alone,
We can steer them from heaven above
And toward my fiery throne.

"And to those who try communing with God
But don't receive that for which they pray,
We'll say, 'Your efforts are foolish.
It's time that you find your own way.'

"It simply comes down to destroying their faith
In conversing with the Father above.
They must believe that he doesn't care,
That they're unworthy of his love.

"They mustn't learn that the Father hears
Every single heartfelt plea,
And when the time is right, he answers,
Once his children fall humbly to their knees."

Secret Nine

The Devil knows the power of prayer,
Which brings us to Secret Nine,
And to keep you from using this precious gift,
There are tricks that he's designed.
But let not the Devil deceive you
Into believing there's no time to pray,
For God has given you no greater tool
To use throughout your day.
The powers of heaven await your call,
Ask and you shall receive.
How many times has this been promised
To those who will ask and believe?
So pray to the Father, ask in faith,
Let not the Devil take this from you,
For prayer is one of the most powerful things
You will ever choose to do.

*Satan's cause is never more in danger
than when a human being,
no longer desiring,
but still intending to do God's will,
looks around upon a world
from which every trace of God
seems to have vanished
and asks why he has been forsaken,
yet still obeys.*
—C. S. Lewis

Chapter Ten

Obedience

*As the Devil paced, his minions could sense
There was more he wanted to say,
But he'd never been at a loss for words
And they were stunned by his display.*

*Then he stopped and glared at his spawn,
Sending chills up their backs.
He hissed, "There's a principle above all others
That we must mercilessly attack.*

*"Obedience to God's commandments
Is the first rule of heaven above,
And from it flow the laws and the prophets,
Including the greatest law, love.*

*"We must make obedience seem
Like a burden too heavy to bear,
And once we've put this into their hearts,
We can easily lead them from there.*

*"We know that one of God's greatest gifts
Is the freedom he's given man,
So we must twist this right to choose
And bind every person we can.*

*"We will whisper, ever so softly,
'No one should tell you what to do.
Forget commandments; they only hold you back.
Your life should be all about you.'*

*"We'll then suggest they can take a vacation
From doing what is moral and right:
What happens in Vegas stays in Vegas,
Oh, their sins will be our delight.*

*"To think some may actually believe
That obedience comes with a loophole.
This lie is one of my favorite lures
For capturing many a soul.*

*"We'll also whisper, 'Choose what you obey,
Little sins aren't a crime.'
They mustn't learn that life is best
If they obey all the time.*

*"We know God's laws are meant to bless,
To protect his children from sorrow.
So we must promote, 'Eat, drink, and be merry;
Delay obedience until tomorrow.'*

*"And if we do what I know we can do,
Millions will fall for our ruse.
And if we hold them to the very end
They'll be paying the old Devil his dues."*

Secret Ten

*Secret Ten is the perfect example
Of the Devil doing all that he can,
To take the Father's perfect gifts,
And stain them in the minds of man.
Commandment, what a terrible word,
How dare God tell you what to do?
At least that's what the Devil wants
Commandment to mean to you.
But commandments are simply heaven's laws,
Meant to bring us peace and joy,
And happiness comes in direct proportion
To how commandments are employed.
When willingly followed, commandment's fruit
Falls freely from the Tree of Life.
And obeying will open our eyes to see
There's no burden in doing what's right.*

*Let God's promises shine
on your problems.
—Corrie Ten Boom*

Chapter Eleven

Addiction

*Satan appeared to be quite pleased
As he watched his sinister band,
His followers anxiously waiting to hear
What remained of their master's plan.*

*He then said, "Let me speak of a tool,
One that's really quite easy to use."
And as his legion awaited his words,
The Devil was mildly amused.*

*"I call this tool addiction,
And its hold can be tight as a vise.
And when compared to Christ's warm embrace,
Its arms are as cold as ice.*

*"There are compulsions I have inspired,
From whose clutches it's hard to escape.
And if, through them, we ensnare God's children,
The rest of their lives we may shape.*

*"I don't have a favorite addiction,
You'll see, they're all quite effective.
I simply love how they imprison the user,
Which is my ultimate objective.*

*"As always, we'll begin by whispering that
Just once will do them no harm.
Most believe they can escape the trap,
And therein lies addiction's charm.*

*"And as we nudge them through its door,
Before they know it, they'll be locked in.
Yes, I like addiction a lot,
It's a gift-that-keeps-giving kind of sin.*

*"So let me address but two or three
That possess an appealing grip,
And if we use them as I foresee,
From many, their freedom we'll strip."*

Secret Eleven

*In Secret Eleven Satan teaches
That man is a weak little thing,
But there's never been a greater lie;
We're children of a King.
If we fail the Devil will whisper,
"You've fallen, just give in."
But understand that yielding to this
Is the only way he can win.
You truly are a child of God,
With powers you have yet to discover,
And if you stumble the way is provided
For you to fully recover.
Ignore the Devil's whispered lies,
And the half-truths he tries to teach,
And know you can never fall far enough
To be out of your Savior's reach.*

*Although the world is full of suffering,
it is also full of the overcoming of it.*
—Helen Keller

Chapter Twelve

Alcohol and Drugs

*The Devil considered his first deadly vice,
And what a useful tool it has been
Throughout millennia in leading mankind
From God and straight to him.*

*"Alcohol," he said, "oh, that fiery juice.
How many have felt its hold?
The victim believes it's a warm, fuzzy friend,
When in reality it's heartless and cold.*

*"It not only devastates users,
But many of their loved ones, too.
Liquor has brought generations to ruin,
Making our work easier to do.*

*"Many go on living good lives
While imbibing every once in a while,
But it's the millions who can't escape its grasp
That we must work to beguile.*

*"Alcohol will soon take them over,
Until there's nothing more important in life,
And once the old hooch has a hold on them,
They'll neglect child, husband, and wife.*

*"Their existence will revolve around drinking
While numbing their minds to the Comforter,
For how can they hear the Still Small Voice
In the midst of an inebriated blur?*

*"How I love the nature of alcohol:
How it turns many good men mean,
How it leads them away from God
And to a thousand unholy things.*

*"So let's promote this vice to its fullest,
Binding all of God's children we can,
Then we'll continue on our ruthless mission
With addictions for the rest of man.*

"Next," he said, "we will move on to drugs,
To catch the unsuspecting user.
And before he knows it, he'll become
A hopelessly enslaved abuser.

"Some of these drugs are so very potent
That one time is all that it takes
To cause a person to surrender control,
And what follows are a million mistakes!

"To catch them we'll send out a clever lie,
One they'll believe if we use a little tact.
Something to the effect that marijuana's okay,
Just avoid things like meth and crack.

"But it's the supposedly innocent drugs
That lead many to experiment.
And before they know it they're beholden to me,
And in the gutter their lives are spent.

"But if the user just stays high
By doing nothing but a little weed,
Then doing nothing is what often happens,
And that's really all that we need.

*"One of the things I love about drugs
Is users think they have spiritual impressions.
Some even believe they've spoken with God,
When it's really just sin-spiration.*

*"Let us whisper little lies in their ears,
And say it's from heaven above.
While we school them in idleness and mayhem;
Instead of chastity, we'll promote free love.*

*"There are so many things they'll accept
While they're flying high as a kite,
And as drugs smother Christ's light in their lives
They won't see wrong from right.*

*"We must keep their minds so clouded
Through this addiction's insidious pull,
That rather than live lives of great worth,
They spend their lives doing nothing at all."*

Secret Twelve

In Secret Twelve Satan tries to conceal
That the Spirit must be our guide,
That it's a gift beyond compare,
Blessing those in whom it abides.
So beware lest your mind be clouded,
Leaving you unable to hear its voice,
For when left without its holy influence,
You risk making a perilous choice.
Keep yourself so you can always feel
The still, small voice of truth,
Then as hazards approach and decisions arise,
You'll see clearly what you should do.

*You are today
where your thoughts have brought you;
you will be tomorrow
where your thoughts take you.
—James Allen*

Chapter Thirteen

Pornography

As the Devil pondered the many addictions
Used to bind the human race,
So many started out harmless,
Though in the end all would debase.

In moderation most things are fine,
But it leaves a list that never ends,
For whatever pulls you away from God
Is a compulsion he will befriend.

But there's an obsession taking center stage,
One quite old, though in many ways new.
And while pornography's been around for ages,
Through the Internet, it's made a debut.

The Devil said, "We'll say it's just fun,
How can pictures do any real harm?
Though we know that that mistaken belief
Is what gives this plague its charm.

"Pornography has the awesome potential
Of enslaving an entire generation,
And it's quickly become one of my favorite tools
In dragging mankind to damnation.

"For pornography embeds cancerous thoughts
That can lead to terrible actions.
It's a mind disease, quite difficult to heal,
So I'm sure you can see my attraction.

"One little click, one more dark thought,
A new suggestion is all that I need.
For no one knows better than we do,
That man's the sum of his planted seeds.

"Watch the video, read the magazine,
No, we cannot allow them to see
That the proverb speaks the real truth:
'As a man thinketh...so is he.'

*"Man mustn't learn that the harvest law
Will be either foe or friend,
But that ignoring it is impossible
Because it never breaks or bends.*

*"As a farmer will never gather a crop
If he fails to work the ground,
A man will never know virtue
If in him crudeness abounds.*

*"But we'll never say, 'Be careful
Of what you allow in your mind.'
For we know that thoughts can lead them to God
Or to a torment I have designed.*

*"We'll say, 'Thoughts are itty-bitty things,
Here for a moment, then they're gone.'
But if they suppose thoughts are trivial,
They risk becoming my pawn.*

*"For more than face, fingers, and toes,
Man's a collection of his thoughts,
And if his mind wallows in the sewer,
He gives me what I've sought."*

Secret Thirteen

The Devil seeks, in Secret Thirteen,
To take a great thing and make it small,
Because really, what kind of damage
Can thoughts do, after all?
In truth, you are creating yourself
By what goes on in your mind,
And every thought to which you give life
Becomes you by your design.
If your mind dwells on vulgar things
It will unerringly lead to sorrow,
For the dark thoughts that you harbor today
May find life in yonder tomorrows.
But if you choose to plant your thoughts
In beautiful and virtuous sod,
You will become one of the pure in heart
And one day, blessed to see God.

*Never worry about numbers.
Help one person at a time,
and always start
with the person nearest you.*
—Mother Teresa

Chapter Fourteen

Hope

The Devil knows that help waits
For those who've paid addiction's price,
And shepherds have been sent to find them
By the shepherd of all, Jesus Christ.

Our Savior's love is so much stronger
Than the grasp of the Evil One.
So, if you desire to be free,
Come unto the Father and Son,

Like Joseph of Egypt, flee enticement,
Run from the tempter's snare,
For its reward is Satan's abode
And you'll never find peace there.

Yes, the Devil seeks to bind you,
For he wants no soul to be free,
While liberty and joy await you,
In the man from Galilee.

Secret Fourteen

*The call goes out to the shepherd,
"Gather my sheep who are lost.
For every soul is precious to me,
And each was worth the cost."
But in Secret Fourteen the Devil drones,
"You haven't time to search.
There's so much that you need to do,
And anyway, what's one soul worth?"
But unknown to the lowly shepherd,
That while searching the barren ground,
Not only is a lost lamb saved,
But the shepherd is also found.
For every shepherd has once been lost,
Every shepherd has wandered and roamed,
And the miracle is, that in finding lost lambs,
The shepherd is also brought home.*

*I often laugh at Satan,
and there is nothing that makes him
so angry as when I attack him
to his face, and tell him
that through God
I am more than a match for him.*
—Martin Luther

Chapter Fifteen

The Devil

*The Devil said as he smiled,
His eager followers looking on,
"One more thing must happen
To carry out our clever con.*

*"Mankind must come to fear me,
They must believe I'm a potent beast.
And once convinced they're powerless against me,
On many a timid soul we'll feast.*

*"They must see me as a monster,
A great dragon, a serpent, and more.
They must fret until I'm in their dreams,
And the boogeyman outside their door.*

*"And we'll even inspire the media
To make movies and publish books
That glorify me through terror,
Until the innocent and gullible are hooked.*

*"They'll honor me as they panic,
And fear their own shadows as well,
And we'll lead many souls to believe
That heaven is less powerful than hell.*

*"And once they're convinced I'm omnipotent,
That I am impossible to resist,
We'll pull them from their Savior,
And I will reign in their midst.*

*"Mankind must never, ever learn,
That I'm not an all-powerful ghoul,
And what I was allowed to do to poor Job
Was the exception and not the rule.*

*"They must never learn that the first step
To diminishing my perceived authority
Is to simply refuse to listen to me,
And make Christ their first priority.*

"But fortunately, men usually follow
Those who pummel and grind.
It's the stomping on necks that gets their attention,
And rarely those who are merciful and kind.

"So, fear me, fear me, fear me they must,
They must believe I'm an almighty fiend.
Through fear we'll come to own millions,
And from their Savior they'll be weaned.

"Make me the beast that they dread,
The terror that wakes them in the night,
For they must never come to know
That I'm powerless against God's might."

Secret Fifteen

Secret Fifteen is Satan's arrogant lie,
He wants us to see him as he's not.
He's not a great monster for all to fear,
But the hopeless enemy of God.
And the day is close upon us
When the Almighty will decree
That he who was cast from heaven
Will be exposed for all to see.
And in that day we'll marvel,
As we view that shackled being,
At how so many chose to follow him,
Rather than Israel's redeeming King.

*If we are wise,
we will encourage, praise,
and exemplify everything
which invites the companionship
of the Holy Ghost.
—Henry B. Eyring*

Chapter Sixteen

The Holy Spirit

There's one great gift the Father has given.
Though known by many names—
The Holy Ghost, the Spirit of the Lord,
Even the Comforter—it is the same.

As much as anything, the Devil wants you
To ignore this still, small voice,
For it will lead from his wily ways
And toward a better choice.

The Devil will whisper, "It is not there.
It's something you cannot see.
Feelings of peace are just chemical reactions.
Do what you want and I'll make you free."

But he's wrong, because this Spirit
That touches the human soul
Was given on creation's morning,
To guide man and make him whole.

Joy is what Satan denies you
As he thwarts the Spirit's call.
And while he tells you listening is useless,
Its value is truly above all.

For the voice you choose to follow
Will determine your destination.
Will your journey end at the Devil's lair,
Or in a heavenly habitation?

The Spirit's mission is to lead mankind
So they with God become one,
While Satan's desire is to steer you away
From the Father and Holy Son.

Ignore the Deceiver's whisperings,
For the Comforter is as real as you,
And if you have a heart that truly feels,
It will lead you to all that is true.

Secret Sixteen

The Devil's Sixteenth Secret
Is quite harmful, as you will see,
For he seeks to keep the Holy Spirit
From influencing you and me.
He tries to overwhelm us
With the busy-ness of life,
And instead of joy and harmony,
Promotes pettiness and strife.
But the Still, Small, Voice whispers
Of hope and peaceful things,
Its song, our soul's desire,
Carrying joy upon its wings.
But know that there are forces
Working evermore
To lead you from its guiding light
And toward life's rocky shore.
But the voice that leads you unto Christ
Is the one that you must heed,
For it will guide you safely
Upon life's stormy seas.

*The Bible to me
is the most precious thing in the world
just because it tells me
the story of Jesus.*
—George MacDonald

Chapter Seventeen

The Word of God

*"Mankind has a tool," said the Devil,
"That if used will despoil my plan.
If the Word of God is studied and lived,
We'll lose our power over man!*

*"One thing I loved throughout history
Was that few could read for themselves.
Most were fed what I wanted them fed.
They were ignorant and blind little elves.*

*"Then along came Johannes Gutenberg,
And his infernal printing press.
And what should be his most famous work
But the Holy Bible, no less.*

*"From Gutenberg it only got worse,
God's Word was no longer for the few.
Overnight, everyone had it,
Making our work harder to do.*

*"But all's not lost," said the Devil.
"There's much that is going my way.
Now that the Bible's commonplace,
It's not as treasured as back in the day.*

*"With as worldly as man has become,
We're pulling many away from God's Word,
And instead of hungering after truth,
The treasures of earth are preferred.*

*"If they only knew what feasting
On the Holy Scriptures would do,
Man would lay aside less needful things,
And have their souls daily renewed.*

*"So we must be clever and cunning,
And make use of each and every tool
To ensure they ignore the scriptures,
And do what we want them to do.*

*"For if they sincerely study the Word,
They will unfortunately come to see
Our lies for what they really are,
And we cannot allow that to be."*

Secret Seventeen

*Satan's Seventeenth Secret
Is one that few understand.
He's used ignorance for millennia
To blind the eyes of man.
But now we have the Word of God,
So that each of us may learn,
And if we're to know the Father's ways,
To the scriptures we must turn.
And a sacred gift awaits us,
As we study and seek inspiration,
For amid our searching we'll discover
Unwritten words of salvation.
Unwritten words spoken to our soul
That will lead us to the Father and Son.
Unwritten words, given by the Spirit,
So we, with Christ, may be one.*

*God loves each of us
as if there were only one of us.*
—St. Augustine

Chapter Eighteen

Jesus and You

The Devil hates no one more than Christ,
And yes, he knows him quite well.
And it will be under the Master's hand
That Satan will be bound in hell.

Yet as long as the serpent is able,
He will battle for the souls of man,
For his wish is to make as many share
In his misery as he possibly can.

But our holy guide will protect us,
He's overcome the best efforts of hell.
And his deepest desire is the will of the Father,
Which is bringing us home to dwell.

Christ is the Way, the Truth, and the Light,
And the straight path, he has shown.
Now, will you choose to follow him
So he can make you his own?

The Cross and Gethsemane miracles
May be difficult to comprehend,
But if not for thirty-three sinless years,
They couldn't have happened in the end.

Yet he is the lamb without blemish,
He gave a priceless gift that is free,
And to receive it, accept the invite,
"Come and follow me."

But the Devil will whisper time and again
That Christ is only historic man,
And he will pull all from Israel's King
That he possibly can.

But let not the Devil make you believe
That Christ is less than the Bible reveals.
The Only Begotten Son of God,
The physician who permanently heals.

He will move mountains for the sin-racked soul,
And with joy make the brokenhearted sing.
And if ever you question his perfect grace,
Think of that Road-to-Damascus thing.

There's only one gift you can give him,
All your heart, mind, and soul.
So take your hands away from the wheel
And allow him to take control.

For if you offer your life to Jesus,
You will soon come to see
That your joys will be deeper and sweeter
Than you ever imagined they'd be.

It won't be a life void of trials,
That's not the path he trod,
But it will be a life that leads you back
Into the presence of God.

He will magnify all the days
That you willingly give to him,
Until your cup is filled with joy,
Even overflowing the rim.

You must admit, it's a pretty good deal,
That in giving your all you receive
Everything that the Father hath,
And a joint heir with Christ you will be.

Yet the Devil will try and have you believe
That you're simply biological man,
That your earthly walk is happenstance
And not part of a grander plan.

How dare you think it possible
That you're anything special at all?
A child of God? How preposterous!
You're just another brick in the wall.

"Eat, drink, and be merry," he'll say,
"This life is all that you've got.
Either serve or take advantage of others,
In the end it matters not."

But again he's wrong, yes, ever so wrong,
For you are a precious soul.
And the very one who created all
Gave his life that you might be made whole.

Would the Father sacrifice his begotten Son
For something that's simply a fluke?
If questions persist, ponder his message,
In Matthew, Mark, John, and Luke.

Yes, God views each of his children
As a pearl of infinite worth,
And to one day return to his presence
Is your reason for walking this earth.

As the challenges of life beset you,
And the Devil whispers, "All is lost,"
Gird your loins and fresh courage take,
For your soul was worth the cost.

The precious blood has already been spilled,
It's time to accept the gift.
Will you be a tare or a kernel of wheat,
When the Master comes to sift?

Know that the Father loves you,
Have eyes that you may see.
Accept Jesus as your very own,
And in heaven with him you'll be.

Refuse to heed the Devil's deceit,
For you are God's precious child.
When you were born you were known by him,
And heaven's angels smiled.

But with billions walking this great big world,
How can such an idea be true?
Yet, therein lies the miracle,
And that miracle is you.

Secret Eighteen

It almost feels like blasphemy,
The very thought a sin,
That our Savior gave his life
So we may be joint heirs with him.
How can such a beautiful truth,
Such a merciful doctrine be,
Such perfect charity extended,
To such an imperfect you and me.
Yet selfish Satan seeks to hide
Deep in Secret Eighteen,
The reality of our Savior's love
And the greatness of his being.
It's no surprise that selfish Satan
Wants to hide our Master's grace,
For the sole intent of selfish Satan
Is to pull us from Christ's embrace.
Yet joy is our promised legacy
Eternally at our Savior's side.
The price is paid, the gift extended,
Now accept that you may abide.

*How art thou fallen from heaven,
O Lucifer, son of the morning!
How art thou cut down to the ground,
which didst weaken the nations...
yet thou shalt be brought
down to hell, to the sides of the pit.
They that see thee shall narrowly
look upon thee, and consider thee,
saying, Is this the man
that made the earth to tremble,
that did shake kingdoms;*
—Isaiah 14:12, 15–16

Chapter Nineteen

The Devil's End

*The Devil adjourned the training
Of those employed in his terrible cause,
All who, in a day that was soon to come,
Would be damned under heaven's laws.*

*They'll never know joy, never know peace,
They've forfeited the Father's love,
And for their rebellion they've been banished,
Eternally, from heaven above.*

*The only success Satan can know
Is that he will not suffer alone,
For there will be souls without number
Surrounding his terrible throne.*

*What a hideous creature he must be
To want to bring so many down,
Simply to satisfy an eternal rage
And bring luster to his filthy crown.*

*But as always, the power is yours,
You must choose what you're going to do.
And remember, if Satan draws you his way,
Permission Came From You!*

Secret Nineteen

The last of the secrets is not so secret,
The Devil is going to fail.
And through our Savior, Jesus Christ,
Righteousness will prevail.
But what the Devil wants to hide
Within Secret Nineteen
Is easily found as you open your Bible
And read John 3:16.

D. Brooks Baker and his wife are the parents of of five children, and currently reside in northern Mississippi. He attended college in California and Idaho and has worked in manufacturing management for two decades.

But it is Baker's experiences as a missionary and Sunday school teacher that inspired his novel The Devil's Secrets. Writing on and off over the years, one morning he awoke with the first chapter running through his mind—and it all seemed to rhyme. Even though it wasn't his typical style, he wrote down the beginning and never looked back. He hopes that by revealing the Devil's game plan through fictional verse, readers will learn to clearly see the obstacles in their lives and be inspired to overcome.

Made in the USA
Charleston, SC
03 January 2014